In Mexico

by Elena Martin

STECK-VAUGHN

Harcourt Supplemental Publishers

www.steck-vaughn.com

Contents

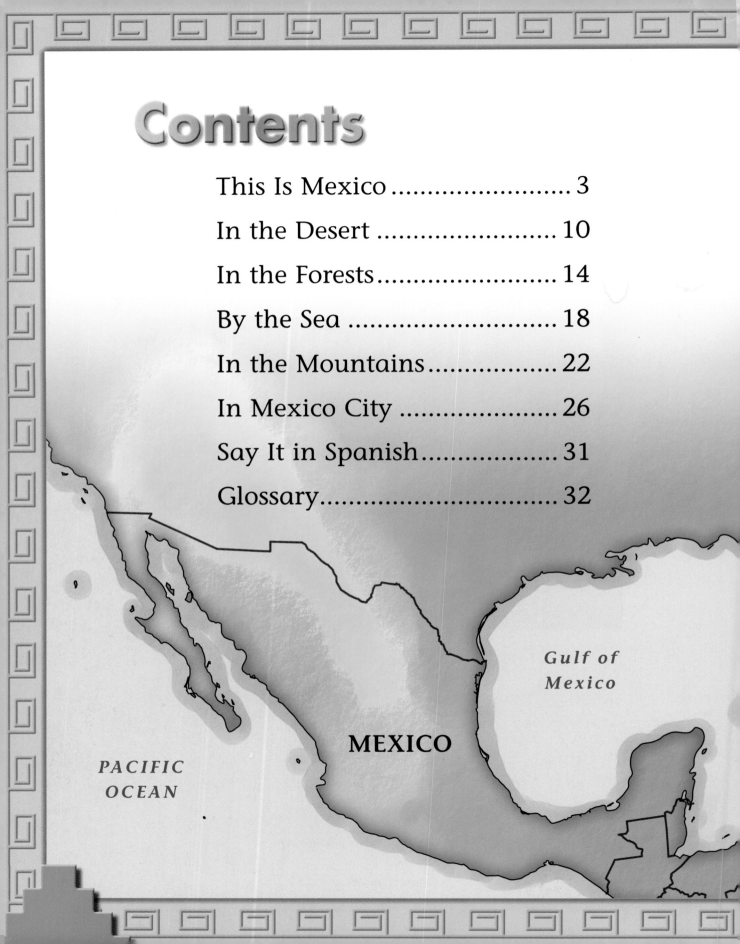

PACIFIC
OCEAN

MEXICO

Gulf of
Mexico

This Is Mexico

These children live in Mexico. Mexico is a country in North America, just south of the United States. What do you think your life might be like if you lived in Mexico?

If you lived in Mexico, you would probably live in a city. Most of Mexico's people live in cities. You would go to school from about eight o'clock in the morning until about two o'clock in the afternoon. All of your lessons would be in **Spanish,** because that is the main language spoken in Mexico.

Children in a Mexican school

A family enjoying their afternoon meal

After school, you would go home to eat with your family. In Mexico, the afternoon meal is often the biggest meal of the day. Adults and children come home from work and school to be together. When the meal is over, you might rest before playing with your friends or helping out at home.

The Mexican flag

Long ago, most of the land that is now Mexico was ruled by the **Aztecs.** The Aztecs were a group of Native Americans who built great cities there hundreds of years ago. The eagle and snake in the middle of the Mexican flag today are from an old Aztec legend.

Very old Aztec buildings

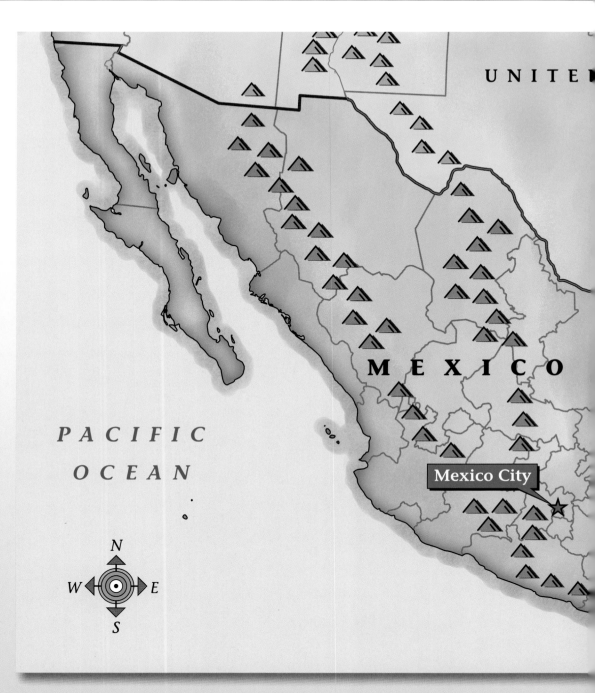

Mexico is a very big country. It is made up of 31 states. Millions of people live in Mexico's cities, but some Mexicans live in small villages or on farms.

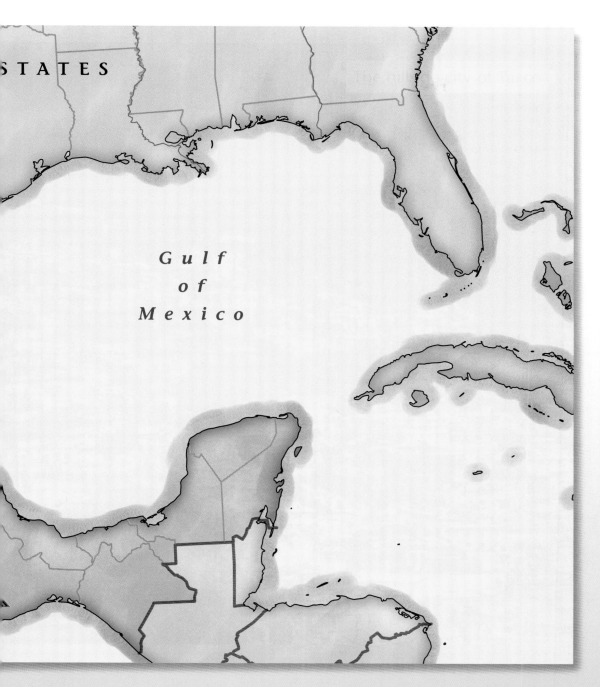

STATES

Gulf
of
Mexico

Mexico also has tall mountains, **rain forests,** and deserts. Not many people live in these areas.

In the Desert

Almost half of Mexico is covered with desert. Few people live in the desert. Why? It is too hot and too dry! There is very little rain. The land is sandy and rocky.

A dry Mexican desert

There are very few trees. But there is life in the desert. Cactuses and other plants grow there. They can live in the dry heat without much water.

Javelina

Animals live in the deserts of Mexico, too. Some of the animals, such as **javelinas,** get their food and water from desert plants. Gila woodpeckers look for food in tall cactuses.

Gila woodpecker

Other desert animals hunt for their food. Snakes and coyotes search for rabbits and lizards to eat. Watch out for scorpions! Their sting is poisonous. Scorpions eat mainly insects and spiders that scurry through the desert.

Rosy boa

Scorpion

Coyote

In the Forests

Other parts of Mexico get much rain. More plants can grow in these parts of the country. Tall, strong trees grow in the thick rain forests. Large wild cats called **jaguars** snooze on tree branches.

Jaguar

Basilisk lizard

Quetzal

Many other kinds of animals live in the rain forests of Mexico, too. Hundreds of different kinds of birds make their homes in the trees. Some forest animals, such as the basilisk lizard and the tiny red-eyed tree frog, are hard to see. They blend in with the leaves and flowers.

Tree frog

Monarch butterflies

One forest in Mexico gets some special visitors every winter. Once a year, **monarch** butterflies fly to this forest all the way from Canada and the United States. The butterflies spend the winter resting in the pine trees.

A farm in Mexico

In the past, much more of Mexico's land was covered by forest. Over the years, many trees have been cut down for wood. Farmers have cleared land to plant crops. Today, the Mexican government has made laws to protect the forests.

By the Sea

Mexico also has thousands of miles of **coastline,** or land by the ocean. Along this coast lie some of the world's most beautiful beaches.

People who live near the ocean get used to hot, sunny weather. It is a good thing they can go in the ocean to cool off!

A beach in Mexico

People come from all over the world to visit Mexico's beaches. The oceans around Mexico are home to many colorful fish, coral, and other animals.

Scuba divers near the coast of Mexico

Some people swim with **scuba tanks** and masks that help them breathe while underwater. Then swimmers can get a good look at the ocean life in the water below.

In the Mountains

High above the beaches are the many mountains of Mexico. It can get very cold up in the mountains. Some of the tallest mountains are **volcanoes.** Some of these volcanoes have not erupted for hundreds of years. Others have erupted more **recently.**

El Popo, a large volcano in Mexico

Bighorn sheep

Mountain lion

Some of the mountains are so rough and rocky that people cannot climb them. There are very few roads through these mountains. But many animals make the mountains their home. Bighorn sheep and mountain lions can climb the mountains easily.

Cities and villages can also be found in the mountains of Mexico. The city of Taxco sits on the side of a mountain. Taxco is famous for its beautiful old buildings and hilly streets.

The hillside city of Taxco

Taxco is also famous for its silver. For hundreds of years, miners have found silver in the nearby mountains. Artists use the metal to make beautiful things.

In Mexico City

Mexico's capital is one of the biggest cities in the world! It is also the oldest city in all of North America. Mexico City has tall buildings and busy city streets.

Mexico City

Very old Aztec buildings in Mexico City

About seven hundred years ago, the Aztecs had their capital city on this very spot. Amazing Aztec buildings are still part of the city today.

A park in Mexico City

If you lived in Mexico, you might take a boat ride in the largest park in Mexico City. This park was first used by Aztecs hundreds of years ago.

The National Palace of Mexico

The National Palace is another special place in Mexico City. The president of Mexico works here. The Mexican flag flies over the entrance of the palace.

Mexico is a country of many different things—deserts, forests, beaches, mountains, and cities. If you lived in Mexico, you would be very proud of your home!

Say It in Spanish

adios (ah dee OHS) . . . . goodbye

amigo (uh MEE go) . . . . friend

buenos días (BWEN ohs DEE ahs) . . . hello

comida (coh MEE dah) . . . . afternoon meal

escuela (ehs KWAYL ah) . . . . school

fiesta (fee EHS tah) . . . . party

gracias (GRAH see ahs) . . . . thank you

por favor (POHR fahv OHR) . . . . . . please

Glossary

Aztecs — Native Americans who once lived in the land that is now Mexico

coastline — land next to the ocean

jaguars — large wild cats

javelinas — small animals that are somewhat like pigs

monarch — a kind of butterfly

rain forests — forests that get much rain

recently — not very long ago

scuba tanks — tanks that hold air for people to breathe underwater

Spanish — the main language spoken in Mexico

volcanoes — mountains or hills that have openings in the ground from which hot gases, lava, and ashes can escape